Owning It

It's my story & I'll share if I want to

Natalie Mangrum

First paperback edition October 2019

Book design by Guglik Design
Editing by Renee Hill
Author photographs by Jessica DeLeon

ISBN 978-0-578-54188-4 (paperback)
ISBN 978-0-578-56826-3 (ebook)

nataliemangrum.com

This book is dedicated to my Pap, who never missed a track meet and caught me every time I jumped into the air from his living room stairs. I'll see you soon.

And to Chris—God's greatest gift to me.

Contents

Introduction

I got the idea for this mini-memoir while on the massage table at my chiropractic office. I often do a lot of thinking during these appointments because, well, I've never been one to relax and shut off my brain. I've always envied people who know how to meditate and "focus on the breath." As I lay there, my eyes started to flutter. I'm talking a vigorous, unnecessarily extreme flutter. For me, that's a sure sign that my brain is like, "OMG we have an idea!!!" I could feel it happening and I couldn't stop it. My massage therapist surely noticed it too, because she kept telling me to breathe. As much as I tried to breathe and relax, the idea kept flowing. The message was clear: We have a story to tell. Actually, we have several.

When I finally got off the table, which felt like forever by the way, I texted three of my friends. These were the same three friends who I spoke to when I first had the idea for my company, Maryland Teacher Tutors in 2015. I always,

always, always run my ideas by people I trust. I don't always get the response I'm hoping for, but I do it anyway. I like to verbally process and hash out the things I'm thinking through. This particular group of friends was super supportive then (when MTT was just an idea) and they were super supportive now. They told me things like, "People love stories of triumph!"

"This sounds like a book full of testimonies and I love testimonies!"

"Girl you got this—a memoir is a great idea!"

Once I got home, I wrestled with two doubting beliefs before I sat down to write. One, I'm not important enough to write a memoir because who do I think I am writing about my life at 34? Two, who do I think I am writing about my life at 34 when I'm not important enough? I decided that this book is less about me than it is my desire to share some of the valuable lessons I've learned along the way, no matter how young. And also, I've been doubted before, by myself and others, and that's never stopped me.

Of course once I actually started writing, all hell broke loose. I ran into all kinds of random, but maybe not so random obstacles that only served as further validation that I needed to get these stories out. So, here we are. If you haven't taken the time to look at the description on the back of the book, you really should. Are there actually people in the world who don't read the descriptions? How in the heck do you know what you're getting into?

If you're part of that group—this is for you:

> *I grew up in the suburbs with two amazing, loving, married parents. So how did I end up dropping out of college (I went back later and finished), getting pregnant at 20 (just missed being a teen mom statistic), and later marrying a divorcee who already had two children? I'm not saying that any of this is bad or can't be mitigated, I'm saying that it wasn't part of "the plan." In spite of my obstacles—and there were many—and against the odds, I went on to become the founder and CEO of a successful, rapidly growing company. In this short and synthesized version of my life, I talk about some of my poor choices, the horrible things people have said (and done) to me, and how I attribute my success to my faith and relentlessness. There is power in sharing your story. When you own your story, you accept what was done to you or what you brought onto yourself, you deal with those emotions, and you make the decision to move forward. You will not stay stuck. And when you allow yourself to be vulnerable and share your truth with others, you pave the way for others to heal.*

I need to admit that my writing is not very pretty or fluffy (as if you haven't already noticed). I never did well with fiction in creative writing courses. But I excelled in professional and academic writing. I write the same way that I talk. It's mostly direct and to the point and if details are added, it's because they're important for context. There's no flippin' way anyone is going to get a novel out of me. Ever! I'm basically giving you the major pieces of my 34-year-old life in a book you can read within the hour.

Feel free to read this book in whatever way you choose. You bought it, after all! It's yours. Don't be afraid to peruse the chapter titles and skip ahead to the good stuff. But in my opinion, this book is best read from beginning to end. My upbringing and my growing up in youth group will make more sense when you get to the rape and infertility sections of this memoir.

Writing this small memoir was therapeutic, but also difficult. There were parts of my story that I had stuffed away somewhere, and bringing those memories back up made this book an emotional process that I wasn't expecting. During the writing process, I suffered intense stomach knots from the stress of regurgitating past hurts. I am grateful to my husband for his love and patience as I spent some time away in hotel rooms and kicked him & the kids out of the house so I could have peace and quiet.

I've included reflection questions and lessons learned at the end of each chapter because I don't believe we were meant to walk through things alone. I believe that there is camaraderie, unity, and oftentimes healing when we share—even if sharing is done between you and your journal. That's a start! Learning more about one another and sharing stories serves as a great reminder that we don't have to walk through life's journeys alone. On my blog over at www.nataliemangrum.com, I'll be discussing each chapter in more detail and I would love for you to be part of the conversation.

My hope for you in reading this book is two-fold. One, I want you to get to know me better. Share in my joys, but also my burdens. Know that I am a person and all of us are a lot more alike than we think. Two, I want you to walk away feeling inspired, motivated, and hopeful. Whether that inspiration drives you to do an extra load of laundry, seek out therapy, or start your own business, I pray you make good choices—and know that you are loved, even when you don't.

CHAPTER 1

My Suburban Upbringing

I grew up in the suburbs with two married parents. I don't think that should be taken lightly. I once heard a man on TV say, "If you grew up in America, you hit the lottery. If you grew up with both parents, you hit the jackpot!" I had stability. I didn't go back and forth. I didn't live in two separate houses depending on the day or week. I had consistency, both in expectations and in consequences. There was no manipulating of mom or lying to dad because they were both very involved in my life. And they were always on the same team. I was nurtured by my mom and inherited a hard work ethic from my dad. With that said, it's also worth noting that I had no shortage of functional men or women in my life. My grandparents were around. In fact, I spent the majority of my elementary years with my Pap and Grandma before and after school. Being raised by two happily married parents helped to set me up for success.

The only thing missing from my upbringing was the white picket fence. I had married parents. Check. I had a big front yard. Check. I had a dog. Check. My parents are amazing, and they did a phenomenal job raising me and my two siblings. I don't say that because I'm awesome—that would be weird. I say that because that's the consensus of our extended family. *Gib and Vanessa did good.* That's what I've heard from aunts, uncles, and cousins. It's no wonder because my grandparents are equally, if not more amazing. My paternal grandparents literally lived in the same exact neighborhood as us. Before and after school, my siblings and I walked to our grandparents' house, which came with—you guessed it—a good marriage and a big front yard. Oh and The Price is Right, of course. If my retired grandparents did nothing else, they definitely never missed an episode of The Price is Right. My maternal grandparents lived roughly 20 minutes away, but I saw them often since my grandmother was basically our nanny during the first five years of my life. When she drove us around, she sang hymns and catchy spiritual songs that she basically made up off the top of her head. I cherished her love and her wit. When we were afraid to drive over bridges, she told us "Don't ever be afraid of water. Water is blessed. Jesus was baptized in water." When we were scared during thunderstorms, she would tell us, "Rain is good and necessary. It

wipes away the dirt and grime that builds up on the streets."
We spent minimal time in my grandmother's house because
she believed that staying active kept her young and spry.
We were constantly running errands and traveling to spend
time with family and friends. I know that having two good
sets of grandparents makes me a blessed woman. I don't
take it for granted.

My parents had the three of us close together. We were all
in college at the same time. I'm the oldest, my sister Kristen
is the middle child, and my youngest brother, Michael, is the
baby. On the outside, we all seem quite similar. My mother
modeled how to "fake it to make it" incredibly well. If she
had a bad day at work, you wouldn't know it. She answered
the phone in the same cheery voice every time it rang, and
you wouldn't be able to tell the difference between her
mood if she won a million dollars or her dog died. She was
the woman at the restaurant and grocery store calling the
server and cashier by name and making conversation with
them. She always kept a pleasant disposition and the three
of us are the same way. But underneath the outer shell, we
are all very different. My brother is creative and artsy, my
sister may as well be re-named Susie Homemaker, and I'm
always focused on the next big thing, challenge, or achievement. My husband describes my brother as charming, my
sister as loving and humorous, and me as mission-minded.

My sister and I fought something terrible growing up. We still do if we're around one another for longer than five days. As adults, we've realized that space is a good thing, and while we love spending time together, we also love *and need* our time apart. Neither of us fight with my brother. He refuses to play into our drama. My siblings and I are very close. I guarantee the two of them were the first two people to purchase my book. Whenever I check my Instagram stats and insights, my mom, sister, and brother lead the way in likes and comments. They are my ride or die people for sure.

Ninety five percent of the people in my family are married to the same person they had children and raised a family with. When my cousin got divorced, we were all shocked. It was just not something that happened in our family. Life was good. We had few complaints growing up and thought that everything and everybody was fantastic. Problems and issues were never talked about. We were sheltered. In fact, I remember my godmother telling my parents one day that she thought it was strange that we had never heard of or been to The Hill District. In Pittsburgh during the time that I was growing up, this was an impoverished area riddled with crime. My parents saw no need to expose us to this, and so they didn't. I would never ever blame my parents for sheltering us. But only God knows if it ended up backfiring later in life.

My parents have always been supportive. Even now, as I am making the choice to take a deep dive into sharing my story and allowing others to be part of it. I'm sure my parents aren't jumping for joy or giggling over coffee about this decision. My immediate and extended family is the type to keep secrets locked up in a closet and let the cobwebs get cozy with them. They see no reason for tragedies, poor decisions, and shameful circumstances to make it out into the open. Nevertheless, I know they understand what I am trying to do by opening myself up to the world. And they are 100% behind me.

I thank my mom and dad often for raising us and doing a damn good job. They usually respond with, "We did the best we could with what we knew." Isn't that the heart of all parents? I think the way my parents set boundaries and protected us was wise. But it's possible that my rainbows and gumdrops perspective of life growing up is one of many factors involved in some of the poor decisions I would make later in life. You just keep reading and judge for yourself.

***

Reflection questions:
How would you describe your upbringing? How has it molded you into the person you've become?

What this experience taught me:
An amazing upbringing does not guarantee a life without pain and it certainly does not guarantee a life without bad choices.

CHAPTER 2

Youth Group

I was raised in church. I know that statement is relative because being "raised in church" runs the gamut of people being in church 3–4 times a week, as well as those attending church once a month and considering that as regular attendance. When I say I was raised in church, I mean my family went every Sunday, no matter what. We were the family that didn't celebrate Halloween because it was the "Devil's holiday" so we dressed up and ate candy at church on Halloween instead, and called it Family Fun Night. If I go back to my old church on any given Sunday, I guarantee I will know all of the words to all of the songs they sing, and I've been gone for 20 years. My old church is nostalgic for me. It's traditional. It's timeless. It's home.

My youth pastor and his wife were like a second set of parents. In addition to spending every Sunday with them from 9:00 a.m. until 1:00 p.m., we spent a lot of time in their home and on youth retreats every summer for weeks at a time. If I think about them for too long, I am bound to get teary eyed because they taught me the love of Jesus, how to live for Him, and to be honest with myself and others about my struggles. Shout out to Reid and Mikki! I still have their house phone number memorized because they told us to call them if we ever got ourselves into a situation that made us uncomfortable, no matter the time of day or night. That's the kind of people they are.

I feel very strongly that my church upbringing kept me from getting into more trouble than I did. And I feel confident that my early memorization of Scripture and constant interactions with the truth of who God is helped to sustain my faith when life got particularly difficult. There is also no doubt in my mind about where my blessings come from. On a panel for a prominent women's conference in Maryland, I was asked how my company grew so big, so fast. I answered, "The Lord." One lady applauded. Everyone else just stared at me, wondering if that was the title of a new podcast or book.

My hope for my children, now 17 and 15, is that their foundation of being raised in the church will sustain them. Right now, they don't always make good decisions. Neither did I at their age. I know that Truth is being taught to them, both at home and at church, and I am confident that as they age, those timeless Truths will carry them, and be a constant reminder of Who is for them, no matter what they do or don't do.

***

Reflection questions:
Were you raised in church? If so, how did that experience shape you? If not, what philosophy or way of thinking molded you into the person you've become?

What this experience taught me:
Train up a child in the way he should go, and even when he is old, he will not depart from it. Proverbs 22:6

CHAPTER 3

Middle School Changed Me

My husband is mildly uncomfortable with how comfortable I am around men. When given the choice, I will choose a conversation over drinks with men over a conversation over tea with women any day of the week. Let me be clear: I love being a woman and I love other women. I just don't tend to enjoy what women are known to talk about in group settings. I'm not going to talk about my kids, I'm not going to talk about shopping, and I'm not going to talk about my favorite recipes. What I will talk about is my revenue projections for the company, how bourbon is good for your health, and why the Jeep Cherokee is better than all of the other SUVs. I blame middle school for this.

Once upon a time, I was a girl who loved spending time with other girls. I laughed with girls. I jumped rope with girls. I trusted girls. And then one day, a really mean group of girls decided to make me the target of their hatred. I thought these girls were my friends and they turned on me in ways that still break my heart all these years later.

When I turned 30, I wrote a letter to my 12-year old self. Here it is:

Dear Natalie,

You don't know this yet, but middle school is going to be very rough for you. Your closest friends will turn against and betray you and you will be left all alone. You will walk the hallways bearing the shame of being abandoned and mistreated and no one will come to your aid. During this time, you will spend hours in the bathroom after school praying to God for help. You were taught He is the only one who will never forsake you. You will cry a ton.

In high school, you will have a group of friends, but you will always be sort of an outsider. In your friend group of five, two of the pairs are best friends- you are like a fifth wheel—not paired with anyone. This will end up being your pattern in life. You will always consider yourself an outsider when it comes to close female friendships. You don't know how to be a good friend. Yet. You put up a wall after what happened to you in middle school and so you keep most women at a safe distance.

Right around your 10th grade year in high school, your friendships with men will always be closer than your friendships with women. This is likely the result of your middle school years. You will find that men are easier to hang around than women. They don't typically betray one another, their friendships are relaxed and less likely to have drama, and you have fun with them.

I want to advise you not to build up such a strong wall after being betrayed. Just because that group of friends abandoned you doesn't mean all of your friends will. Learn what you need to learn and be wise. But stay vulnerable. Jesus knew Judas would betray Him and yet, he spent time teaching and loving him. You may have missed out on some amazing friendships by not letting your guard down around women.

My middle school experience changed me. We all have events or circumstances in our formative years that mold us into who we are. This chapter is short, I realize that. All these years later, I think it is still a sensitive spot for me, and I'd rather not think about it too deeply. My mindset at this point is: It happened. It almost ruined me. I wish it wasn't part of my story.

***

Reflection question:
Can you think of an experience from your child-
hood or middle school years that changed you?

What this experience taught me:
Our tendency to build walls is our way of pro-
tecting ourselves so that we survive. It is not a
bad thing. It is how God made us. But recog-
nizing those walls and working towards tearing
them down to be more human and open to love,
should be the goal.

CHAPTER 4

College Dropout

I jumped from middle school to college because nothing truly eventful happened during my high school years. I had a long-term boyfriend who I was engaged to who later went on to play in the NFL. I made good grades, I bought new clothes, and I consistently found new ways to cut my hair and keep it spunky. See, nothing's changed. Still the same ol' Nat. When it comes to my college dropout experience, it went a lil' something like this:

It was the beginning of my sophomore year. On the first day of class, I decided to sleep in and not go. I figured the only thing the professors would do is give out syllabi and force us into silly introductions to pass the time. But then I didn't go the second day. And I didn't go the rest of the week. Instead, I slept in and hung out at the snack bar during lunch, but that really wasn't so fun since all my friends were in class.

I had no sense of direction. I felt like I was wasting my time at school since I had no idea what I actually wanted to do as a career. At the time, I was a communications major and I only picked that because it seemed like I could do a lot of things with that degree. After two weeks of missing class, I decided I wanted to go home. I had enough sense to know that if I left early enough, I could get an incomplete instead of a failing grade; and I knew my parents could get half of their money back if I left before midterms.

So, I emailed them.

Yes, you read that right. Let me take a brief detour about my choice to email them.

In March, I was a podcast guest about financial literacy and entrepreneurship called Econix Talks. When I told the host, Josh, that I sent my parents an email about dropping out, he died laughing! After I explained that there was no way I was telling my Black parents over the phone that I was dropping out (for fear that they would've hung up and driven 1.5 hours to my dorm room), he understood. In my mind, an email was a way to soften the blow. They would read it separately, then together, and sleep on it. And that's exactly what happened.

My mom responded with a one-liner about how she was sending my dad and uncle up to get me that weekend. And that was that. When my dad and uncle arrived, my uncle pleaded with me not to leave. "Please don't do this Nat. Please." I felt like such a failure and a disappointment. His words ripped my heart open, but I stuck with my plan to go back home and find a job. On the way home, my uncle continuously tried to change my mind while I wept silently in the back seat.

Back home in Pittsburgh, I found a job doing data entry and it was horrible. It was eight straight hours of typing on computer keys. It was torture for a woman whose idea of patience is waiting longer than five minutes at the nearest Chipotle. Last week, my husband shared a list of things he loved about me. Patience did not make the list. He knows it. I know it. We all know it.

When people hear that I dropped out of college, their first response is, "What?!" That is then followed by, "Wait, weren't you a teacher?" Let me be clear. I dropped out. And then I realized it was a cruel world out there, so I went back. In fact, I couldn't wait to go back! I'm sure my parents laughed hysterically at how badly I suffered during those out of school months. They couldn't wait to kick me out when I decided to return to campus the following semester. Little did I know; the upcoming years would be far from easy.

***

Reflection questions:
Did you attend college, and do you feel it is necessary to have a degree in today's world? What are the main reasons you are for or against higher education?

What I learned from this experience:
It's never too late to change your mind and switch directions once you realize you've made a bad decision.

CHAPTER 5

College Campus Outcast

Almost as soon as I stepped foot onto my college campus of Clarion University as a freshman, I took notice of the Black fraternities and sororities. I had gone on a Black college tour as a senior in high school and was vaguely familiar with the camaraderie of these organizations. I knew immediately that I wanted to be an AKA. Who wouldn't want to wear pink and green and be a distinguished woman of Alpha Kappa Alpha? I never even considered a different sorority. The AKAs were known as being pretty, scholarly, and desirable—and that's what I wanted to be. When they walked through parties, they held up imaginary mirrors! It might seem silly now, especially if you're not familiar with or involved with Black sororities. But to me, this was life! I thought joining would make me noticeable and popular. So, I did. I was an AKA for a little over a year before I completely denounced the sorority. Whoa, you must be thinking.

Where did that come from? Let me explain.

The camaraderie was great. The bonds I made were amazing. The friendships were second to none. But to be quite frank, I was weirded out by some of the stuff that happened during my initiation and ceremonial processes. Because I had grown up going to church, my conscience was extra sensitive. And I've always had intense gut instincts when it comes to things. I knew I couldn't stay involved in this organization and have a clear conscience.

But I may not have gone about leaving the organization the right way.

My denunciation was extreme. In general, my personality is pretty black and white. I've been known to be one of two things. Detached and cold, or "extra" and dramatic. There is not usually an in-between. But this was super extreme, even for me. I threw away all of my paraphernalia, I deleted contacts out of my phone, I called the corporate office and told them to remove my name from the directory, and I told the Sorors in my chapter to remove all of my information from the website. But here's the kicker. It wasn't enough for me to leave the organization and leave other people alone to make their own choices. Oh no. I basically shouted from the rooftops that all fraternities and sororities were evil and that getting out was the only way to be free. At the time, I absolutely believed that you couldn't be a Christian and in a sorority. The two were oxymoronic. As I write this, I'm shocked that people from college are still friends with me.

This is one of the things I regret most when I look over some of my life experiences. I made some great friendships being part of Alpha Kappa Alpha and I ostracized myself by refusing to have anything to do with anyone who didn't agree or listen to my rants. As I continued in this vein, I lost lots of friends and in general, when people saw me coming, the Red Sea parted, and I was gawked at. "She's a weirdo" and "She's completely gone off the deep end" were common phrases I heard uttered as I walked to and from my classes. Plus, the only two friends I had left kept me updated on the recent gossip about me. I mostly kept my head down until graduation and was able to make some friends from the gospel choir to keep me from going completely dark.

***

Reflection question:
Have you ever intentionally or unintentionally ostracized yourself for something that seemed really important at the time, but looking back, wasn't that serious?

What I learned from this experience:
Being extreme is fine, if that's what you decide is best for you. One could even argue that it's necessary at times. But I learned that there are usually more effective ways to go about things that don't involve losing friendships or causing unnecessary relational tension.

CHAPTER 6

Almost a Teen
Mom Statistic

Despite my knowing and believing that sex outside of marriage was not God's intention, I did it anyway. I bet there are a lot of people reading this who can relate. Those teenage hormones are a bear and college made it so easy since there was so much freedom and autonomy. I was off and on with my high school sweetheart in the earlier years of college, but towards the third and fourth years of undergrad, the relationship dwindled completely. Not long after, I started dating a new guy. He was fun to be around, I loved his dance moves, and he was part of a fraternity that my friends and I often hung out with. We traveled together to other college campuses to party, and we often took the 1.5-hour drive back home to Pittsburgh on Sundays during football season because our families were (and still are) die hard Steelers fans. Side note: I don't know anyone from Pittsburgh who isn't a die-hard Steelers fan. But I digress.

Funny enough, we ended up denouncing our Divine Nine fraternity and sorority around the same time, so he became quite the comrade and confidante to me. His denunciation was either because I was super convincing about why our organizations were evil, or he felt bad for me. Either way, I didn't feel quite so lonely and isolated with him around, and we enjoyed the time we spent together. Maybe a little too much.

After about a year of being together, I went to the doctor for my annual Pap smear. When the nurse finished taking my urine sample, she came back into my room and told me that the doctor wanted to speak to me. "About what?" I asked her. She never responded—just smiled and gently closed the door. When the doctor came in, she asked me if I was aware that I was expecting. "Expecting what?" I asked.

"You're pregnant," she told me.

"Surely you're mistaken. I've been on Depo Provera for a year."

"Well, there are a small percentage of women who get pregnant, even while on birth control."

Great, I thought. *Just my luck. The church girl who recently denounced her sorority for the cause of Christ is pregnant. What a great witness for God you are, Natalie.* I asked the nurse to get my boyfriend from the waiting room.

When my boyfriend entered the room, I told him the news. And to my surprise, he had the biggest smile I had ever seen. *How dare he?! Was he happy about this? Did he want this to happen? Was he insane?* A few days later, I accepted and embraced the news, despite knowing that my life would be a lot different. I suppose it was better to have a boyfriend who was excited than to have one who might suggest or push me toward an abortion. So, thank God for that.

During the Christmas holiday, my boyfriend and I went back home to Pittsburgh. My boyfriend's parents responded favorably. They told us they wish we had waited, but that the baby wouldn't want for anything and that they were excited. They themselves had been teenage parents so perhaps they wanted to show us grace and love instead of disappointment. My parents, on the other hand, were devastated. My mom didn't speak to me for months and my dad suggested I get married because that was "the right thing to do." I had a sneaking suspicion that my boyfriend and I would not make it if we got married so I opted to respectfully disagree with that advice and instead, take things one day at a time. My mom cried every night while I was pregnant and to this day, I've never spoken to her about it in depth. This is how it works in my family. I assume she had certain hopes and dreams for me, and she must've been heartbroken that this decision had made my life much more difficult than it needed to be.

After the winter break and holiday was over, I arrived back at school and continued my life as normally as I could. I went to class, kept my work-study job, and went to track practice every morning at 6:00 a.m. and every afternoon at 3:00 p.m. I started to show around week 16 so it was obvious to the people who knew me on campus that I was expecting. I bled off and on throughout the pregnancy, but the doctors assured me that it was normal to have a little bleeding every so often. Nevertheless, every time it happened, my heart stopped. Blood and pregnancy are not a good combination and I wrestled with whether or not this baby would be ours to keep or if something was wrong.

Around week 20, I was bleeding heavier than normal. It was the middle of the night and I woke my boyfriend up to tell him. We called his mom and she suggested that we go to the emergency room as soon as possible. When we got to the rural emergency room in our college town, the doctors were upfront with us that the baby had a heartbeat, but that we may want to consider going to a hospital closer to home to have family support. We packed a few things and headed back to Pittsburgh around 3:00 a.m. On the drive home, I remember listening to Smokie Norful's song, *I Need You Now*. I felt so at peace and ultimately accepted in that moment that whatever happened, I would trust God.

I started bleeding again while in the car, so rather than go back to campus, we decided to go straight to an emergency room in our hometown. I'll never forget what happened after I put on my gown and had my ultrasound. The ultrasound technician looked at me with a heavy sadness in her eyes. I asked her if there was a heartbeat and she said that the doctor would be in to speak with me shortly. I knew what that meant. My baby was dead. My boyfriend walked angrily into the hallway to cry and punch the air. I sobbed until the doctor came in and confirmed what I already knew. He informed us that because I was so far along, they would need to do surgery to remove the baby from my womb. I would have to go under anesthesia, and they wanted to do it as soon as possible to prevent the risk of infection.

Both sets of our parents, as well as my godparents, arrived at the hospital promptly. As I prepared to be wheeled out for my surgery, a different doctor walked in. He put his hand on my hospital bed and said, "I don't know if you're a believer, but Romans 8:28 says that all things work together for the good of those who love God and are called according to His purpose." This same Scripture would come to mind again and again during different seasons of my life, but none of the upcoming times would be quite as impactful as this one. I still remember exactly what that doctor looked like and what clothes he had on under his lab coat. His face, his words, his tenderness, are forever etched in my memory. Sometimes I wonder if he was an angel sent to comfort me and remind me that God is with me, even in my poor decisions.

My family gathered around me and said a prayer before I went under anesthesia and when I woke up, they were all waiting for me. The doctor mentioned something about the surgery being a difficult one because of how far along I was and muttered something about my cervix and scraping; but he assured me that things looked okay. At the time, I didn't pay much attention to what he said. I was heavily sedated with anesthesia and glad the surgery was over with. I looked forward to grieving and gaining some closure. Years later, when I found out I couldn't carry children, that doctor's comments would haunt me.

***

Reflection question:
Have you ever experienced miscarriage, infer-tility, or something along the same lines? For example, I have a friend who grieved not being able to have children due to chronic illness. Her body was capable of having a baby, but it would have ruined her health.

What this experience taught me:

Sometimes life sucks.

CHAPTER 7

Rape

I've always assumed the best in people. To this day, I would consider myself an optimist and the only reason I am more apt to check my surroundings and not trust whatever people tell me is because of my police officer husband. He has tried to teach me that there are people in the world who like to harm others. My man is a straight shooter. "You're a soft target" he would tell me. "You're a woman and you're petite. It won't take much effort for a large man to knock you upside the head and rape or kill you. So be alert and be prepared." *Well alrighty then. Now that that's settled, I guess I'll just continue to live life feeling good and safe. Not!* My parents definitely taught me to be careful, but they never went into detail about stranger danger and rapists and murderers. That just didn't happen where I grew up. With the exception of middle school, I completed my K-12 education mostly unscathed by the ills of the world. It wasn't until college that life got really painful and confusing.

During the night of my rape, I was still in "goodie two shoes" mode as a newer Christian. I didn't go to campus parties anymore and on this particular night, there was a big event that I had chosen not to attend. Lots of alumni had come in for this party that one of the fraternities was hosting. My boyfriend was working an overnight shift at a nearby restaurant. A mutual friend of ours asked if he could crash at my apartment that night since my boyfriend was working and unable to let him into his place. "Of course," I told him, "you're always welcome here." That night, I went to sleep around 11:00 p.m. I sent a text to our friend to let him know that the front door was unlocked, and I had made his bed up for him in the living room with the pull-out sofa. The layout of my one-bedroom apartment was pretty typical for the off-campus housing on campus. When you walked in using the front door of the apartment, you were immediately in the living room/kitchen area. If you were to continue to walk straight back, you would be in front of the door that led to the bedroom. That night, our mutual friend arrived at my home around 2:30 am. He never stopped in the living room. He knocked on my bedroom door, which was locked, and I woke up to open it, thinking he may have needed some additional bedding or wanted a glass of water. What followed was a nightmare and for the sake of my husband, my parents, and my children who may one day read this, I am choosing not to go into the details of that night. Suffice it to say, he raped me.

When the individual left (who I will hereafter refer to as Pity instead of "our mutual friend"), I called my boyfriend and told him what happened. He left work and on his way to my apartment (unbeknownst to me), he called my father and shared the news. (It took me years to forgive my boyfriend for doing that without my permission, but that's another story for another day.) During this time, I received pages and pages worth of text messages from Pity. He went on and on about how sorry he was. I held onto the messages long enough to show my boyfriend and then later deleted them. Seeing them in my phone made me sick to my stomach.

I went to college about an hour and a half away from my hometown and exactly 1.5 hours after I shared the news with my boyfriend, my mother was at my door. It was 4:30 a.m. I suppose I should have felt comforted, but I was mortified. I was in a very vulnerable place and I really wasn't ready to be held, discuss what happened, or file a police report. I just wanted to cry alone at my boyfriend's house because I didn't want to be in my own apartment, and I didn't want to be home by myself. My mom signed me up for therapy. I went once and didn't like it, so I never went back.

I went on with life as best I could. I graduated with a 3.9 GPA and went on to grad school. To this day, I'm not sure how Romans 8:28 ("For we know that all things work for the good of those who love Him and have been called according to His purpose") applies to that situation and if it even makes sense to try and find a lesson in it. What I do know is that I became more suspicious of people in general, even those who proclaim themselves as friends. I suppose I've learned to be a lot more careful now that I've had first-hand contact with people who wish to do others harm. I am pretty proud I graduated on time and with such a great GPA, but I do blame Pity for my 3.9 GPA when I was definitely capable of a 4.0.

***

Reflection questions:
Have you been through a traumatic experience? Lots of things can cause trauma—it doesn't have to be rape. Miscarriage, divorce, infidelity, loss, chronic pain, a car accident, etc. How did you get through it?

What this experience taught me:
You don't have to find a lesson in rape. It's utterly terrible.

CHAPTER 8

Marriage and New Motherhood

This was one of the more difficult chapters to write. In the other chapters, I can choose to be as transparent as I want, without involving other people. But this part of my life includes my husband Chris and our two children, so I have to tread more lightly in order to protect their experiences. If and when they're ready to tell their stories, they will do that in their timing.

If you've kept up with me at all in the past couple of years, you'll notice I am careful not to call my children "stepchildren" and not to call myself a "stepmom." By definition, those labels are true of me and true of my children. But in my love and actions, they don't begin to identify who the kids are to me, nor do they identify the two particular roles to which I've been called. Moms who adopt don't refer to their kids as "adoptive-kids." They call them their children. I'm not sure why society deemed it necessary to interject a specific word for "step-kids" who didn't come from your body, but I'm not here for it.

My children know I refer to them as my daughter and my son when we are out in public or people ask what their relationship is to me. They've been through divorce, which is a heartbreaking nightmare for kids at any age. I would never seek to alienate them further by implying that they aren't fully part of this family. My parents and siblings feel the same. When someone asks my mother if my sister's 1-year old daughter is her first grandchild, she says no—without hesitation—and proceeds to identify our children Natasha and CJ as her first two grandchildren. Let me rewind a bit and give some backstory to my relationship with my children and how it came to be.

When I first met Chris, I was immediately attracted to him. I mean, he is gorgeous. We were both part of the same church and at the time, our church had 17 members. The church was brand new and everyone except the pastor was under 30. So, we hung out often and got to know each other very well. I quickly realized that Chris had two children, but there was never a woman with him. Not at church, not at Bible study, not when we all hung out. This was not necessarily unusual, however. I thought she may have worked on

Sundays or didn't care to come to church. After a few Bible studies, Chris shared his story. In order to protect our children, I won't share the details of why he and his ex-wife split up, but in a nutshell, they were headed for divorce and Chris was raising the kids alone.

If I'm honest, the fact that Chris had kids was a deterrent initially. He was so handsome, so fantastic, so everything I wanted—but I knew even then that blended families were tough for all involved, and I didn't think I was ready for that commitment. As much as I tried to not fall in love with Chris, God had other plans. He and I both agree that we were drawn to one another in a way that felt outside of our control. There is no other man on Earth who can be to me and for me, what Chris is. He's perfect for me. And I know that without a doubt. Our dating relationship was short. We dated for nine months and were engaged for three.

When Chris proposed, he showed me a photo of him and the kids when his ex-wife first left them. He spoke about how devastated they all were, and how by me coming into their lives, they felt joy again. Even then, he wanted to be sure that I knew a commitment to him meant a commitment to the children. I said yes! And I knew what I was signing up for when I did. But that certainly didn't mean that this new life I was beginning wouldn't be difficult.

When Chris and I got married, the kids were 8 and 6.

They had gotten to know me well before then because of our heavy involvement in the church. I've never been afraid to tell the kids that being a stepmom was difficult for me. They understood, because being a stepchild with two divorced parents is even more difficult. We all took part in counseling and therapy, and I pray our family is better for it.

There are a number of reasons why being a stepmom is difficult. I'm not planning to list each of them out and take up your precious time. Just know that the job is hard! And even though I knew what I was signing up for, I could never have prepared myself. And let me be clear: It's not my children that made it hard. I know that is the case for some blended families. For me, it was the combination of being a newlywed and a new mom on the exact same day. I was used to my space and used to getting up and going whenever I wanted. I frequented happy hours, traveled often, and spent my money however I pleased before I got married. Similarly, I didn't have time to carry my children, prepare for their arrival, build a nursery, create a bond, and watch them take their first steps. I was immediately thrust into motherhood and expected to know what the hell I was doing with two small humans! My life changed dramatically. My money went to child support, happy hours were replaced with caring for the children, and traveling was much rarer because of our childcare schedule with Chris' ex-wife. In addition to this new way of life, which I was totally unprepared for, Chris and I found out that we were unable to have children (more on this in Chapter 9). That, my friends, was the icing on the cake, and the reason I considered taking my own life in that season.

I threw myself into classes, resources, blogs, and journaling to cope with this new way of life. Some of the blogs I came across were angry, but to be honest, it felt good to know I was not alone. Others lacked depth and seemed to only speak to families who were trying to blend their kids with their spouse's kids. That wasn't my situation and I didn't like being grouped into that category. Parents who already have children and married another person who had children, did not have the same experience as me. To some degree, their freedom was already gone. I went from independent, fun-loving, traveling, single gal to married with kids. My kind is much rarer in the world of step-families. Other resources I looked into kept throwing out this idea that seven years was when experts and blended families believe their families started to feel somewhere close to normal. When you're six months in, seven years feels like a LONG time.

Despite how difficult this transition was, I persevered. But if I'm keeping it all the way real, none of the resources were very helpful. I had to work that struggle out on my own and felt mostly isolated during those several years. Nevertheless, I am beyond grateful that my husband was an anchor during this time. He loved the children and loved me simultaneously and effortlessly. It was never difficult to tell him how I really felt. He always supported me. He often thanked me for choosing to give up the life I loved, to be with him and become part of his family, as hard as it was. And I appreciated his acknowledgment that the job was hard.

There isn't really an end to this chapter because my life married to a man who is divorced and embracing two children is still unfolding every day. But I will leave you with some thoughts I came across from a journal entry I wrote a few years ago:

> *You've heard the adage: If I knew then what I know now... (insert all of the things you would have done differently here).*
>
> *For those of us who believe, we know the truth. God has ordained our every step. Each circumstance, each bout of pain, each glimpse of joy, is perfectly in line with what His purpose is for us.*
>
> *Nevertheless, I enjoy entertaining the thought of what I would have done differently if I had known then what I know now. If I had been given the opportunity to re-route or change course, I like considering*

what things I would have adjusted.

If someone had shown me, at age 26, that marrying my husband would be a sort of "nail in the coffin" of any comfortable and pain-free life, I'd like to think I would have listened. Or at least given proper consideration to the weight of what I was getting myself into.

If I knew then that painful perseverance would be my lot—that life would be an uphill battle each day, I may have opted out. If I knew then that the children's biological mom's disdain for me would transcend any hate I thought I knew about before, I may have graciously passed on the offer. If I knew then that we would be childless because in God's goodness, He decided to withhold babies from us, I may have questioned what it was I really wanted out of life.

But I'm here. And I'm still standing. By His grace.

God has given me some lessons over the years. Heart wrenching lessons dripping with tears of despair. And those lessons have made me better. Those lessons have made me into a woman of substance. Depending on the day, of course.

1.) **Set boundaries.** *Any stepmom I've ever come into contact with had some form of basic amicability with bio mom. Not us. If I knew then what I know*

now, I wouldn't have tried so hard to have a cordial relationship. I would have held her at arm's length-and kept her there. It would have saved me from a lot of disappointment and confusion. Creating distance in volatile relationships is healthy—it doesn't make you weak.

2.) **There is another side.** Suffering sucks and step-parenting is a day in, day out form of suffering for a variety of reasons that won't be covered in this journal entry. Things may not get better the way you think they will. The kids may never respect you; bio mom may never behave the way you think she should, and you may be upset every single time the large chunk of money leaves your bank account. But there is another side. If I knew then what I know now, I would have a seat and rest in what Scripture says about trials. God uses them to change us.

3.) **Take the high road** (or at least make your best attempt). Hold your tongue and don't speak ill of bio-mom. Not just in front of the children, but in front of everyone. God's grace and forgiveness extends to her, too.

4.) **Endurance is a beautiful trait.** 6 years ago, when I was engaged and hopeful and naive, I didn't know how to truly endure. My life had not been too hard yet. But now that I've walked through some different forms of suffering, step-parenting being the *most consistent, God has given me grace to endure other things. Things that would have rocked my world and wrecked me 6 years ago are the same things that push me toward the cross now. I have better stamina. I walk through suffering with a better attitude than I would have. If I knew then what I know now, I would try harder to look to The Lord and what He's doing, rather than wallow in self-pity.*

***

Reflection question:
We all face challenges, obstacles, and trials in this life. Can you think of one that has been chronic? One that is there, staring you in the face, day in and day out, and you can't go longer than a few hours, without being reminded of it.

What this experience taught me:
Life is hard for everyone, albeit in different ways. Share your burdens. You shouldn't walk through things alone.

CHAPTER 9

Infertility

As a little girl growing up, my worst fear was that I would not be able to have children. That is not a normal fear for a child. It's always interesting to me when I look back on my childhood and remember how terrified I would be at the thought of not being able to get pregnant, carry, and raise a child of my own. Was God preparing me for this reality at an early age? I've also wondered if my obsession with not being able to have kids somehow infiltrated my mind and subconscious, which caused my body to reject children. I know the latter is a bit extreme, and I know it's not right to blame myself. But these are the things that used to roam around in my head. None of my other friends recall having those kinds of thoughts as kids. It's an anomaly, for sure.

Once I got pregnant in college while on birth control, those early childhood thoughts of not being able to have children stopped haunting me. Obviously, I could get pregnant! And once I passed the 12-week mark of the first trimester, I was sure I would be a mom in another 24 weeks. I never once second guessed that my pregnancy would be successful. I felt great, I was healthy, and I was young. The doctors had no concerns that my pregnancy wouldn't be viable, and things would likely go as planned throughout the course of my term.

Welp, that obviously wasn't the case.

Despite losing my first child, who I named Jason, I was still hopeful. Maybe losing my son at 20 weeks was some freak accident that wouldn't happen again. Maybe I wrestled too hard with my boyfriend when we had pillow fights. Maybe I shouldn't have gone jogging or continued attending track practice. Maybe I ate too much ice cream late at night. I concluded that there was an odd reason that something went wrong, and it would be fine to try again once I was married. Whew! Nothing could have prepared me for the infertility struggle I was about to endure. Noth-ing!

Chris and I started trying for children about a year after we got married. And by trying, I mean, I started to actually track ovulation and learn about my body's fertile signs. Before that, we were together so often that tracking ovulation didn't matter because we had every time of the month covered. I was sure we should have been pregnant after trying for so long, so we went to see a fertility specialist. They did some preliminary tests and when our blood work came back, they told us that it would be very difficult for us to have children without fertility treatments. I cried on the spot. And I pretty much cried every single day after that for three years straight.

After losing three babies in the womb (my husband says it was five—maybe I repressed the others) and completing **several** infertility treatments, having biological kids didn't happen. It's one thing to know you're infertile for a specific reason. It's a whole other thing for every doctor in every fertility clinic this side of Maryland, to tell you that they have no idea why you're not getting pregnant or staying pregnant. Despite the fact that the doctors assured me that I was healthy with tons of high-quality eggs, perfect Fallopian tubes, and the best-looking uterus they'd ever seen, we were unable to have kids. And we tried everything.

I really did want to be a mom. When I was asked as a little girl about my dreams and aspirations, I simply stated that I wanted to be a wife and a mom. I wanted six kids—all before age 30. In fact, one of my college boyfriends was disturbed that those things were all I wanted.

"Don't you aspire to really make a difference?" "Don't you want to do something inspiring and amazing, rather than ordinary?"

"Nope," I told him, "That's what I want and that's how I

envision inspiration and amazement to look."

Needless to say, that relationship didn't last long.

Believe it or not, I'm okay now. In my mind, our time for children has passed. When we got married, my stepchildren were 6 and 8. Now they are going on 18 and 16. When they were little, I could more easily picture our full home, with small children running around. The gap between the ages of all the kids (step and bio) wouldn't be terribly significant. We would get through it and we would enjoy all of our bundles of joy. But now, after parenting children through various stages of life (including rebellion—one of my personal favorites), I'm okay. I've now gotten used to a clean house, sex in the living room, and random dates to dinner or the movies without having to think through a sitter. Of course, this could all be my mind's way of accepting my reality, and not feeling so bad about it. But what I've lost in the inability to have children, I have gained in an outstanding marital relationship with my husband. We have a real depth in knowing one another. I would honestly argue that my husband and I know one another better than older couples know one another. People who have been married 30+ years. I'm not saying that's the norm. But I'm saying I value what I have in my marriage. I value where we are financially. God doesn't give us too much, but He also doesn't give us too little. We have a beautiful home in a beautiful neighborhood. I worked three jobs when we were first married, and my husband worked two so we could get out of $70,000 worth of debt and work toward financial freedom. This life I know has been riddled with pain, but also abundant with blessing. I've come to accept this life. The reason I never seriously considered adoption is because the thought of embarking on the unknown with an adopted child felt risky. Too risky for someone who wanted to drive into a brick wall and considered using her husband's gun to commit suicide just three short years ago.

Yes, there was a time when we wanted kids. Desperately. But God didn't give them to us.

God's ways are mysterious and His plans for us were different. I think there will always be a small curiosity, a small wish that things had turned out differently. But I trust God and I really do believe with all my heart that He knows my pain. And that gives me real peace. Because I don't believe that He lives to crush me. I believe that His desire is for me to know Him. More intimately. More fully. And I'm okay with that. In fact, knowing Him and walking with Him has brought great joy to my life—and my pain has allowed me to experience God in ways that I just wouldn't have gotten to without suffering.

During those awful years, people said really stupid and hurtful things to me. "Girl, you'll get pregnant! Just relax."

"You're stressed. Have some wine and you'll get pregnant right away."

"Just put your feet up after you and your husband make love. That's the best way to make sure the sperm meets the egg!"

"You're not pregnant because of the food your generation eats. The quality is lacking and it's definitely the reason you can't conceive."

My favorite was when a woman I knew told me that she knew how I felt (at this point I had been trying for four years) because her baby was 3 months and she was having trouble getting pregnant a second time. She couldn't believe it was taking so long. Three months of waiting. Are you kidding me? Y'all—I wanted to assault her.

But I've come a long way since then. I remember squeezing my husband's hand when diaper commercials came on. When I got texts from my newlywed friends about their plans to conceive in 1–2 years, I would think to myself: *Surely we will have kids by then, too.* But with every passing year, we were left without children of our own. In fact, all of the couples who were once infertile have gone on to have children. Except us. The vicious roller coaster cycle of hope and devastation with each new ovulation week and period was like living in a nightmare. I hated my life for torturing me this way, and I hated myself for failing at the one thing women are supposed to be able to do.

I couldn't bear the public sharing of pregnancy news because I couldn't hide my tears the way I could when the news was given via Facebook or Instagram. As much as I wanted to pretend I was happy, I ached on the inside and lived on the verge of constant tears. On one occasion in particular, a woman shared her pregnancy news with the church. She talked about how they had tried for a few months with no luck, but in month five, they had finally gotten pregnant. I burst into tears and it happened completely unintentionally. I was embarrassed and heartbroken that I couldn't share in her joy, and I was horrified that my uncontrollable tears made her moment about me instead of her great news.

I made unsuccessful attempts at avoiding questions about when we would have children from family members on holidays.

When I tell you I cried at night. I mean it. Every. Single. Night.

For three years.

I cried so hard that I often had to leave our bedroom so that I wouldn't keep Chris awake.

But Psalm 30:5 says joy comes in the morning. Of course that's not literal. It doesn't mean that you will go to bed weeping and wake up perfectly okay. But there is joy for the Christian even in the midst of trials. Yesterday morning, I smiled at how cute the babies were on the diaper commercial. This afternoon, when my friend texted me that she plans to conceive again in August so that her children are a perfect two years apart, I felt pleased that another baby would soon be on the way. I LOVE the public sharing of pregnancy news now. It's exciting!

This is a far cry from where I was several years ago.

When family asks about whether or not we will have children, we tell them boldly that we have two. And they're awesome.

I still cry sometimes. But it's a lot more rare. And it's never about the inability to have children.

Though I could go into detail about all of the hormone shots, all of the tears, and all of the physical and emotional pain & heartache that happened as a result of desperately trying to have children when my body refused to cooperate, I won't bore you with the details.

The point is: I'm on the other side. That pain was a dense forest to walk through. Sometimes I didn't walk at all. I crawled. Sometimes I couldn't crawl. I just laid still. But by God's grace, I made it.

As long as I have my right mind, I don't think I will ever, ever, ever forget what it was like to be there. But I do look back on those years with a gentle smile.

God changed me in that trial. I wouldn't be me without it.

Being on the other side doesn't mean that I don't still think about what could have been and feel a twinge of regret about not trying harder, not adopting, not looking into different doctors and methods. It means that *it doesn't consume me*. It means I'm able to move on from the thoughts, accept that God's will was done, and persevere in this life, full of trials.

***

Reflection question:
What is the hardest thing you've had to walk through in life, thus far?

What I learned from this experience:
I am much stronger than I give myself credit for. That experience almost took me out. But here I am.

CHAPTER 10

Too Many Glasses of Wine

In therapy, my counselor asked me what my earliest childhood memory was. It didn't take long for me to share what happened to me when I was a Kindergartener in Mrs. Auhl's class. We were working on a project with dinosaurs. The instructions called for us to match up corresponding letters and numbers and use a pushpin to hold them together. The completed project would be a dinosaur whose arms, legs, and mouth were hinged and could therefore, move like a walking, talking dinosaur. Sitting next to me was a ginger haired child named Tommy. Tommy completed his walking talking dinosaur in a few short minutes. I couldn't quite seem to get the hang of how to work the stupid pins and I became very frustrated. Finally, my broke-down dinosaur was completed. I was not happy with how he turned out.

On the way home from Kindergarten that day, my Pap tried to make small talk with me, and I didn't give him much in the way of my responses. Like always, he asked me to take out the papers from my bookbag at the kitchen table once we arrived at home. Reluctantly, I pulled out the dinosaur. "Let me take a look at that," he said. I handed it to him, feeling angry all over again. "It's beautiful," he said. "No, it's not! It's ugly!" I screamed, before throwing the sorry excuse for a dinosaur into the trash. Tears welled up in my eyes and no matter how many times my Pap repeated that the dinosaur was fine, I didn't believe him.

This was just the beginning stage of my tightly wound personality. I would become mildly obsessed with achievement and accomplishments, and I would have high standards for myself. Despite other people's praise, my outcomes needed to satisfy my standards, or else they were considered failures. It was around this time that I began believing that my value and my worth was solely dependent on my performance. I needed to maintain an image of success and perfection. I believed that if I did not do things well, I would not be accepted. And that's what happened that day in Kindergarten. I felt that everyone at my table, including red headed Tommy, was disappointed with me. I felt that my teacher, Mrs. Auhl, was disappointed with me. I felt ashamed and afraid that I might be found out for the fraud that I was. Of course, the reality is that everyone at my table was most likely focused on their own dinosaur and Mrs. Auhl was probably just happy that we were quietly working. Any time you give scissors to a class of Kindergarteners, you're bound to have a solid 30 minutes of peace. Cutting takes a lot of concentration for the "littles."

In my head, everyone knew I had failed. And most importantly, I knew I had failed.

As life went on, I became the best at everything I attempted. If I knew walking into a situation that there was a chance I would not be the best, I would focus my efforts elsewhere. I was only interested in participating if I knew I would dominate. It's really quite pitiful, but hey—this book is about honesty and vulnerability. I knew I was a fast runner growing up, so in middle school, I joined the track team. I won every sprinting medal there was from middle school to college, and to this day, I still hold the sprinting record for my university. I barely made an effort at practice and sometimes it made me sad to watch other girls work really hard to be fast, and never succeed.

This type of mindset is not healthy and it's not sustainable. I am obviously aware of this and wish I could change. But habits that are created so young are hard habits to break. I experience burnout on at least a monthly basis and my sister, who is an RN, worries that I will make myself ill and have heart trouble if I don't get control over this. I have made myself plenty sick over the years. You can read more about my chronic panic attacks in Chapter 13. For now, let's focus on how I began a back and forth pattern of abusing alcohol when my burnout was at its worst.

I didn't drink much in college. If there was a party on campus, I might have thrown back a shot or two with a group of friends, but it's not something that was part of my life outside of the occasional "pre-game" drinking. I didn't start keeping alcohol of any kind in my house until I got married, became a stepmom, and fought the back and forth battle of hope and depression as a woman who struggled with infertility. Wine became a relief drink for me. After a long day teaching middle school kids, working an after-school teaching job, and helping my husband obtain his bachelor's degree, I was worn out. Add to this the huge life change I had just committed to marrying a man who was divorced with two children, and an ex-wife who was not favorable to me, and I felt like a crazy person. As beautiful as my children are, and as grateful as I am that God gave them to me, this was a transformative life stage. Prior to infertility, I had never walked through anything so hard.

When I started drinking wine, I found that for a brief moment, life didn't seem quite so difficult. It triggered something in my body that forced me to relax, something

I felt I was incapable of doing without the help of this substance. With wine, I felt like I could confidently walk through the pain because it was a numbing source that minimized the many pressures and heartaches I was facing on a daily basis. It wasn't until later that I realized I wasn't confidently walking through the pain at all. I was only avoiding it and I wouldn't be able to do that forever.

As time went on, I continued to drink and use wine as my automatic relaxation tool. I drank wine in the evenings when I was at home, and I had harder mixed drinks when I was out and about in social settings. Though I definitely came to terms with the fact that I abused alcohol at times, I knew I wasn't an alcoholic but decided to be more mindful of drinking as a coping mechanism.

The turning point for me was when I realized my relationship with alcohol was different than the other people in my life. My husband didn't come home looking for a beer when he had a hard day. My best friend could go to a restaurant and order a soda instead of a margarita. My sister, who has a bar in her home, almost never opened her wine. It was like it was there for show, and she didn't care very much about actually drinking it. When I came to terms with the fact that I sought out and responded differently towards alcohol than those around me, I decided I wanted to reflect on my habit and dig deeper into my motives. Once I spent some time dissecting my behaviors, but more importantly, the root cause of those behaviors, I was able to identify the ways in which I was using alcohol to cope. I learned to address my feelings with healthy coping mechanisms like prayer, talking to Chris, and just generally embracing (or maybe walking through is a better word?) hard times instead of seeking to avoid them through numbing myself.

With the help of God, my husband, my journal, and my trusted circle of friends, I was able to learn how to manage alcohol in a healthy way. I am so very grateful that my abuse of alcohol in those difficult years did not progress into an addiction that I would struggle to come back from. I would be remiss not to mention that if you feel you are turning to alcohol to cope and are consuming unhealthy amounts of it to find relief, numb pain, or find happiness—there are a plethora of resources available to you that pull people out of this dangerous cycle. A simple internet search or Alcoholics Anonymous group is a good start.

***

Reflection questions:
What are some healthy coping mechanisms you implement in your daily life when you are having a tough time? In your journal or on the

blog (if you're comfortable), what unhealthy ways have you coped with your pain?

What my experience taught me:
Denial is only going to make things worse. I came to grips with my "relief drinking" early on and was able to get a hold of it before it got ahold of me.

CHAPTER 11

"You're not a good teacher."

"I'm writing you up. You are not meeting the basic standards of an effective teacher."

"If I saw something worth commenting positively about in your classroom observation report, I would have written it."

"Ms. _____, she's a good teacher. You're nothing like her. This profession might not be for you."

Those were the words uttered to me during my second and third years of teaching under a miserable and mean principal. On the first occasion, when my principal told me she was writing me up in front of my students, I couldn't get through the book I planned to read my class during circle time. Lucky for me, while the tears were welling up in my eyes uncontrollably, one of the learning specialists walked in. I threw the Read Aloud book into her hands and told her I really needed to use the bathroom. As soon as I locked the bathroom door, I burst into tears. I sobbed on my knees with my hands around the dirty toilet in the roach infested lavatory. I never wanted to come out.

I had never been spoken to with such disdain. I did have a situation in grad school where my boss fired me because I was a Christian and her atheist heart couldn't stand to be around me. But she covered it up in lies, and I didn't even bother to contest it because I was graduating a week later. This situation with my principal was different. There was no underlying hatred, at least none that I was aware of, so as much as I wanted to believe she wasn't telling the truth about me, I couldn't convince myself otherwise. *Was I a terrible teacher? What was so horrible about my teaching that my principal would tell me I did nothing right? I had great classroom management. My students behaved well for me. They were making academic gains. What was the problem?*

To this day, I don't know what exactly made that particular principal so mean to me, but after speaking to other teachers in the school, it seems likely that she was just miserable and wanted others to be, also. At the time, I was devastated. I had always considered myself an overachiever. I am a Type A personality. Effectiveness and accomplishments have always been the air I breathe. I did everything

I could to never disappoint people. On top of that, this was the career path I had chosen for myself. And because of her comments, I believed I was terrible at teaching. I went in and out of depression for the next several months as I tried to make sense of this. My self-esteem and sense of self-worth was in the gutter and I felt a general sense of confusion about who I was.

After a few years at that school, I got a new position as a reading specialist in a different Baltimore City School. Under the leadership there, I flourished and got back to being the confident woman I had lost in the years prior. The leadership team was blown away by the success my students obtained under my instruction, and they affirmed me constantly. It was in this environment that I realized how delicate I am—how delicate we all are. I was the same Natalie in the first school as I was in the second. But I lost my sense of self and became a depressed and wilted flower under one administrator, and a revived and blossoming one under another. I realized then that words are powerful. So I started speaking words of life to myself and others in a more intentional way. I believe that my time at New Era Academy in Cherry Hill was one of the reasons I went on to become an entrepreneur. Katrina Foster, Jim Grandsire, Roberta Gary—thank you for seeing something in me that I was too broken to identify in myself. Jess Gartner—thank you for being a listening ear, an inspiration, and a trusted friend. With all of your encouragement and support, I regained my courage and Lord knows I would need it once I stepped into the lonely world of entrepreneurship a few years later.

***

Reflection questions:
Can you remember a time where someone spoke words to you that were harmful? How did it affect your sense of self-worth?

What this experience taught me:
I need to know who I am at all times. As a daughter of the King, I need to prioritize what He says about me, first and foremost. Constructive criticism is good for us, but there's a way to evaluate it in light of who I know myself to be and protect myself from it if it is untrue or bred in lies. It takes discernment to know the difference.

James 1:5: NIV: "If any of you lacks wisdom, you should ask God, who gives generously to all without finding fault, and it will be given to you."

CHAPTER 12

MTT—"That's a terrible idea."

I feel like I've told this story a million times. Honestly, I'm tired of talking about it. Retelling how people were unsupportive of Maryland Teacher Tutors when I first had the idea is exhausting. I always want a nap after. Funny how the body is so connected and what affects us emotionally often has a physical effect as well. Despite how tired this story makes me; I know that there will be someone who reads this and finds the courage to go after their dreams in spite of the naysayers.

Here's the full story behind the birth of Maryland Teacher Tutors. I'll share how I started, why I started, where we've been, and where I hope we're headed. But I'll also share about the obstacles I encountered as this dream struggled to be a reality, especially since my challenges came in the form of people, more than anything else.

First things first: I never set out to be an entrepreneur.

I always imagined moving up in the ranks as an educator. First, a teacher, then a team lead, then a specialist, and maybe, just maybe, go into school administration at some point. The idea of being an entrepreneur, and a CEO at that, never even crossed my mind. I think if I'm honest, I just never saw myself as special enough, smart enough, or capable enough—but more than that, I think I was sort of programmed to work for "the man." I never even allowed my mind to dream of anything other than being an employee.

In light of this, Maryland Teacher Tutors was not born out of some dream or passion that I had to stick it to the man and work for myself. It happened almost organically and unexpectedly. But upon further reflection, I think I was built for it all along.

Bear with me as I tell the story of how MTT came to be, because I think if you pay close enough attention, you might find that entrepreneurship could be in your DNA as well.

MTT's existence can partly be attributed to a few different situations that I encountered over a period of a few years. I'll address these situations one at a time, and in chronological order.

September 2013: I was hired to work as a reading specialist in the Cherry Hill neighborhood of Baltimore City.

My principal, whom I adored, and still love dearly, trusted my expertise and my judgment from day 1. She basically told me to do whatever I thought was best for the students who performed the lowest on the state exam. In grad school, I was trained to pull students out of their classrooms to give them instruction. But let me keep it all the way real. I never agreed with that approach, so that's not what I did. I asked my principal if she could group the students into batches of 10 students each, and instead of them going to their regular Language Arts teacher, they would come to me. This means I would see them once a day for one hour each, for a whole semester. Because they saw me in groups of 10, I could engage them with activities that would allow them to work collaboratively, but also give them the one-on-one attention they needed since the class size was so small. To make a long story short, it worked!

Here's an excerpt from the Maryland Teacher Tutors website about this very thing:

> Maryland Teacher Tutors was founded by a former teacher, Natalie Mangrum. As a reading specialist, Natalie worked with a small group of students and recognized the value of one-on-one instruction. On average, her students grew more than 2.5 grade levels over the course of just one semester! In fact, the huge academic gains were so significant that those

students entered the mainstream classroom way ahead of schedule. The power of one-on-one tutoring is important. When you couple that with a teacher who is an expert in content and knows how to deliver that content effectively, you've got a winning combination. We deliver results and we are 100% confident in our model. Our data and reviews speak for themselves. You don't want to see your student struggle. And neither do we. Get in touch. We'd love to help.

Now, even though students grew an average of 2.5–3 grade levels each semester, that was just the average. There was one 7th grade student in particular who came to me on a 3rd grade reading level and left my classroom at the end of one semester, reading and nailing 11th grade level SAT questions. This is not a game. This is real. And I knew there was something huge here. The two main takeaways from this in my mind were "consistency" and "one-on-one." But at the time, I wasn't planning on doing anything with that knowledge. It was more or less just a pat on the back for my achievement-oriented personality that I picked the right approach and it worked. I wouldn't really put this together with some of the other things that occurred in my life until later.

March 2014: Chris and I were on a plane coming back to Baltimore from vacationing in Jamaica. On that plane,

I read a book called *The Millionaire Next Door*. That book completely changed my mindset about money, generational wealth, and financial independence. I read it after we finished paying off debt and I pretty much made a decision right then and there that we would do everything the book said. And we do. The book talks about the ways of life for the wealthy—how they live below their means, how they bargain shop, how they invest in things that matter like education and good accountants, and how they buy used cars outright—cash money. At the end of the book, the author explains that one of the best ways to become wealthy is to own a small business. He even gives ideas of which businesses will always be needed. One of the ones he mentions is education, specifically, tutoring. That's when the lightbulb went off. From that time forward, my mind was open to opportunities in a way that it wasn't before. I had always carried 2–3 jobs at a time, even as a teacher. I would teach during the day, and then pick up after-school teaching jobs wherever I could. Teachers don't make much. Surprise, surprise. But my mindset was different. Instead of picking up work wherever I could to make some extra money, I wondered what it might look like to make an hourly wage that could make a bigger difference. When I was connected to a student who needed a tutor, I accepted the job. I didn't know much about private tutoring, and anyone who knows this story, knows that I asked my WASPy (White Anglo-Saxon Protestant) girlfriends if this was a thing.

"Oh yes! It's definitely a thing. We all had private tutors growing up."

So I went for it. To make a long story shorter, I started taking on more students. At one point, I wasn't getting home until 8:30–9:00 p.m. and my husband, who can only make toast, was starting to feel the burden of caring for two children alone, without me. So he asked me to figure something out. I knew I didn't want to turn business down. So, I asked a colleague if she would be interested in making some extra money on top of her teaching job. She said yes! I created a name for my little business at that time.

May 2015: Natalie Mangrum Learning Services was created. I thought my colleague and I would do reasonably well with our new private tutoring business. I had no intention of growing it. My mindset wasn't even on that level yet. But then we started getting more calls for business and those calls were composed of a variety of needs. Eighth grade algebra. Second grade phonics. Eleventh grade chemistry. SAT prep. I hated turning down calls for parents who needed our service. So I continued to add more teachers to the team. Once we got to tutor number five or so, I decided I was no longer comfortable having a sole-proprietorship business where parents were writing checks to Natalie

Mangrum. It just felt weird.

"What if I named my business something that would indicate a team composed solely of certified teachers?" I asked my husband.

"I like it. Let's do it."

October 2015: Maryland Teacher Tutors was born.

Although Chris and I were elated about the idea and honestly shocked that no one had thought of it before us, we didn't get a positive response from everyone. During the first several months of Maryland Teacher Tutors' existence, I did very little in the way of trying to get the word out to gain exposure. I didn't know better. I had no business background and didn't realize networking, advertising, and business strategy was needed. I did basically nothing and waited for the calls. Only the calls didn't come as frequently as I had hoped.

Finally, I joined a peer advisory group and started attending networking events. My peer advisory group was supportive, but unfortunately, that was not the case at networking events. One gentleman in particular asked me what I did and began brutally dissecting the business. I would have actually welcomed his constructive criticism if he hadn't outright told me that my idea was "cute, but not sustainable." "You can't hire teachers to tutor. Your business will never be profitable. You need to hire college students or PhD candidates who are capable but will work for less."

I walked away feeling discouraged and confused. This man was very successful. He had multiple businesses that were worth millions. Surely, he knew what it took for a business to be successful. And maybe I had made the wrong decision. He was not the only person who didn't agree with my business model.

As a private tutor, I was connected with other private tutors from a tutor community I found online. There are so many positive things I could say about this community. I found one extraordinary woman who I am still in touch with today. She was so encouraging and so helpful when I was first starting out and continues to be just as supportive today. She never charged me for advice, she affirmed me in what I was doing, and she never stopped telling me how proud of me she was. She even offered to let me spend a week in her Florida home if I ever needed to get away. She became a true friend. But the rest of that community was not helpful.

Unfortunately, it reminded me of the crabs in a barrel mentality. Instead of believing that there is enough room in this world for everyone to be successful, people were trying to climb over one another to make it, and they were hesitant and cold when it came to offering advice. For example, I connected with a woman from that community and aside from the fact that she tried to manipulate me into paying hundreds of dollars per hour to coach me, she told me that my company model was not sustainable and wouldn't work. This was the second time I had heard that my company was structured poorly and teachers as tutors was not an idea worth continuing.

Do I have more stories like this? Yes. I could tell you five more just like it. But for every naysayer I encountered, I met ten yaysayers. They were mostly my friends and family who knew very little about education and entrepreneurship, but it was still nice to have encouragement and support as a new and inexperienced business owner.

I've been at this for almost four years now. The first year shouldn't even count as a real year since I had no flippin' idea what I was doing and was still working full-time. But years two and three, I worked hard to build a name and a reputation for Maryland Teacher Tutors. And with the recent press and exposure we've had, I am more than proud of what I've accomplished. God is certainly for me. And I hope to honor Him in everything we do at MTT.

Colossians 3:23 ESV "Whatever you do, work heartily, as for the Lord and not for men."

***

Reflection questions:
When you think about your life, are there experiences that come to mind that stand out? Could those experiences be trying to tell you something? Could they be breadcrumbs leading to an idea, a venture, or a lifestyle change of some sort?

What I learned from this experience:
When you have an open mind, you pay more attention to what's going on within you and around you. So, pay attention.

CHAPTER 13

Anxiety and Panic Attacks—My Chronic Thorn

I was barely functioning. My stomach knots were so painful that I couldn't get out of bed. If I had to describe the feeling, I would say it felt like someone was squeezing a large crusty rope inside of my gut. My heart palpitations were so constant that I thought for certain I was going to have a heart attack. My right eye was starting to twitch, my hands were trembling, and I couldn't sleep at all. I was entering my third year of running MTT and we were growing at lightning speed. Because I hadn't created systems and processes early on in the business' history, I was frantically putting everything together way too late. My days consisted of back and forth emails with my accountant, testing out new software for scheduling and payment, hiring, firing, and creating new contracts and documents for the business. On top of this, I was constantly creating and putting out content across my social media platforms to make sure MTT gained exposure and became a well known company. As if all of this wasn't enough, I was still a wife and a mom. So, there was that.

Throughout my life, I've experienced a variety of physical symptoms when I'm under a lot of stress. As a child, I grinded my teeth. When I got to middle school, I began suffering from heart palpitations. In high school, I hyperventilated when I took on too much.

I tried different things to experience relief. I went to counseling, I journaled, I met with my pastor, and I got lots of exercise. Though some of it helped, it didn't help enough. I was still struggling to function.

So when I walked into the psychiatrist's office for the first time, I was sure I would leave out of there without a solution. Once I got into her office, I proceeded to tell her what was wrong with me. Like every other doctor I had seen, I was prepared for her to tell me I was stressed, and I should exercise. She listened to me talk about how my heart was fluttering and I couldn't get my heart rate to go down, even while asleep. How I felt myself trembling at night and my eye was starting to get a weird nervous twitch. How my stomach was in excruciating knots that I had learned to live with, but every once in a while, they kept me from functioning normally. I would spend a few days a month writhing in pain, incapable of doing anything. My husband would order takeout and my kids would know it was just "one of those days." To my surprise, the doctor responded that I was having chronic panic attacks and what I was telling her was not good. My response was shock and disbelief. Panic attacks?! Chronic panic attacks, at that?! I was both relieved and terrified. I was relieved that I finally had a diagnosis other than "go for a run" and I was terrified that I was the victim of a disorder that had the words chronic and panic in the label.

The doctor sent me away with a prescription for anxiety medication and encouraged me to have a glass of wine and take a chill pill. Well, the glass of wine wouldn't be a problem. *But what is a chill pill and where do they give them out?*

After a few weeks with the anxiety medication, I started to notice a change. I stopped arriving to meetings 40 minutes early so I could find a parking spot and not stress about it. I stopped having stabbing heart pain when my husband was driving (because up until this point, I believed I was the only safe driver in the world). I stopped feeling like I had to have a drink before a stressful situation or a networking event. My heart stopped racing and I was actually able to get some sleep for more than 4–5 hours at a time. Was this my new normal?

Ha! I wish.

Several months later, my stomach knots and heart palpitations returned. They weren't keeping me from being functional, but they were very uncomfortable and still slightly painful. Where before the knots felt like a crusty rope being twisted on my insides, these new stomach knots were a relentless gnawing. I reached back out to my psychiatrist and she upped my dose.

Nothing.

I was still having psychosomatic stress symptoms. It was then that I remembered that our Western culture deals with symptoms mostly, and medicates after the fact. Unlike Eastern medicine, we don't typically address the root cause of issues. I knew I needed to identify and address the root problem if I was going to find relief. So I picked back up with therapy and tried to schedule more vacations. One of the phenomenal things I noticed about my heart palpitations and stress knots was that when I booked a hotel room for a night and left my laptop at home, the heart flutters stopped. The knots didn't go away as easily. But I still believed there was something to it. When I went on extended vacations out of the country where there are beaches and palm trees, both the heart flutters and the stomach knots began to regress. On one occasion in particular, I booked myself a two-hour massage. And wouldn't you know it—I felt the stomach knots start to crumble like hard resistant sourdough bread in a person's fingers. They weren't completely gone that day, but I knew for sure something was happening.

I knew I needed to learn more about self-care if I was going to feel better, both physically and mentally. My sister, who works on a cardiology floor as a registered nurse, told me when we were growing up that she was worried about me. And when she became a nurse, she was even more concerned. "It's people like you that end up in here with heart attacks. You need to learn not to take life so seriously."

I wish it was that simple. This was the only life I knew. Ever since my Kindergarten experience in Mrs. Auhl's class, I became overly obsessed with achievement. And when you're achievement-oriented to the degree that I am, you don't typically stop to smell the roses. Your brain is constantly awake and crowded with thoughts. Forgetting to eat is a common issue for me. My therapist tells me that I need to stop and be thankful for my personality, rather than wish it away. It's because of my personality that I get things done. Lack of motivation and laziness are never going to be used to describe me. My husband doesn't complain that the house isn't clean, the laundry isn't done, and dinner isn't made. He complains that I am running circles around him and it makes him feel useless. I need to stop sometimes and be glad that God created me the way He did.

But that doesn't mean I don't still need refining. You'll never catch me reading a book on productivity or motivation. But you will catch me reading books on how to slow down, the art of rest, and the dummy's guide to meditation.

You may be wondering where I am with all of this now. Well, I'm not seeing a therapist currently, but I go back and forth with it. Since starting my anxiety medication, my stress has lessened tremendously. But it hasn't gone away. There are times when I still struggle with the physical symptoms of my stress, even with the medication. Unfortunately, I have not been successful with work-life balance and when given the choice, I'll choose work every time.

My chronic anxiety is a story that is still being written. But I included this chapter in my book because I really do want to open myself up to people who are similar to me, but also different. If you are a meditation queen, please—help a sistah out. If you are a doer like me, but you've found ways to temper those anxiety prone emotions—help a sistah out. If you struggle with chronic anxiety because you are obsessive about achievement, say something! Reach out, let's remind one another that we are not alone, and let's commit to getting healthy together.

***

Reflection questions:
Are you competitive and ambitious, or are you reflective and creative? Are you more likely to focus on meeting goals at the expense of your health and relationships? Or are you more relaxed and likely to prioritize your relationships over your efforts and accomplishments?

What I learned from this experience:
My personality isn't going to change. So I need to figure out what it looks like to be mentally healthy in light of it.

CHAPTER 14

Why Not You?

If you hang around enough people, especially those who talk about energy and the universe (I still don't understand it), you'll hear the phrase "limiting beliefs." A limiting belief is when you believe something about yourself, other people, or the world at large that limits you in some way. It's usually subconscious. You don't actually know that you believe being rich is evil, but you are afraid of money and don't want to make too much of it because deep down inside somewhere, you actually do believe money is bad.

When I founded Maryland Teacher Tutors, I quickly became aware that one of my limiting beliefs was that people would not respond well to me because I am Black and I am a woman. But mostly, because I am Black. From my perspective, White women were still received much better than Black women. So being a woman was a secondary concern. Being Black was primary.

The first time I came face to face with this belief was when I showed a friend MTT's shiny new website. On the "Our Tutors" page, I put myself way down at the bottom, after all of the other tutors. "Why are you at the bottom" she asked? "Well, because I don't want people to not hire us because the owner of the company is Black." "Forget them!" is what she said. (Actually, she used a different choice word, but it was the same idea). "You don't want people like that using your services anyway! Now, put yourself at the top where you belong!" Sidebar: Love you, Jess! And, so I did. But I wasn't comfortable with it until at least a year and a half later when White people started using our services and didn't mind that I was the Black owner.

I thought this limiting belief was dealt with until 2.5 years into the company, when another woman business owner and I were chatting. Somehow, we got on the topic of what MTT's target market is. "Well, to be honest, it's mostly White working moms who hire us" I told her. I felt embarrassed saying it, like it was wrong or shameful that I was Black, and it was mostly White women who were using our service. *Was I a sell-out?* "You should consider getting into the South Baltimore areas," she said. "Fells Point, Federal Hill, Patterson Park, etc." In my mind, the women who lived in those areas were bourgeoisie—they wouldn't want to work with a company that has a Black owner. I expressed this to her, and her response was, "Are you kidding me?! Everyone loves you! And if you need a basic example, White women love Oprah! Why not you?" I was speechless. She was right. Why not me? Why did I feel so insecure about my race and how it would be perceived by others?

I attribute my ability to address and conquer this limiting belief by my two aforementioned friends who were able to see worth in me when I could not. Since then, I've never looked back. I am proud to be the CEO of a company that I built from the ground up, and though I do my best not to make it all about me, I definitely don't shy away from the spotlight. If I receive an interview or podcast request, I'm in! If I receive a speaking opportunity, I'm in! I am incredibly comfortable in front of White audiences now because I realize that I am me, take it or leave it.

***

Reflection questions:
Do you ever feel "second" because of your race or gender? If so, what has that been like for you and what would be a tangible example of your experience? If not, are you aware of another limiting belief that might be affecting you? Some common limiting beliefs I've heard are, "I am not good enough to _____." I will fail if I step out on faith and try _____." "I will

never make much more money than I do right
now." "I could be successful at _____
if _____ wasn't in my way/holding
me back."

What this experience taught me:
Sometimes we can be our own biggest obstacles.

CHAPTER 15

Matthew 6:33

Matthew 6:33 NIV "But seek first his kingdom and his righteousness, and all these things will be given to you as well."

What things will be added you might be wondering? I'm not 100% sure because I'm not a theologian, but I'm going to go with ALL!

If you're not already aware that God is first in my life and the sole purpose in my being here is to love Him and love my neighbor (which includes you and the rest of the world), then I have failed. I have failed at providing an accurate portrayal of who I am and what matters. Nevertheless, if you are reading this now and you had no idea, I am grateful for this opportunity because—well, now you know.

I am completely convinced that God is for me, He has always been for me, and He will always be for me. Because

I belong to Him. Every story I wrote, every experience I shared, every trial I encountered, He was there. As my story continues to be written, I know one thing for sure. If God continues to give me a platform, I plan to continue to put Him on it.

Final Words

You're at the end of my freakin' book! Did you read it in a day? Over a few days? Did it take you three months? Did you like it? Did you hate it? Did it make you sad? Did it make you happy? Let me just say that if it made you happy, there's no way you're happier than I am right now as I write the last chapter of this 18,000-word memoir. I just needed to acknowledge that I actually wrote a book because I never, ever, ever thought I would be a published author. Ever.

Thank you from the bottom of my heart for supporting me. And not just because you purchased and read my book. Thank you to all of you who continue to root for Maryland Teacher Tutors, and affirm me in my role there as a CEO. Thank you to all of you who respond positively to my posts on Facebook, Instagram, and LinkedIn. Thank you to all of you who care enough to stay updated on what I'm up to and seek out ways to be part of the work we are doing in Baltimore.

I really do hope you'll join me over on the blog at www.nataliemangrum.com as we hash out some of these experiences and connect on a deeper level. I've opened up about my joys and my pain. I've shared my story. It's time for you to share yours.

ABOUT THE AUTHOR

Natalie Mangrum is a wife, mom, and successful entrepreneur. As the founder and CEO of Maryland Teacher
Tutors, Natalie hires private certified teachers to go
into families' homes and provide academic support
to students. In 2015, she founded Maryland Teacher
Tutors with one teacher, and has since grown to 35+
certified teachers working under her leadership. Beyond
work, Natalie enjoys spending time with her husband
and two teenage children, kickboxing, and learning
all she can from people with more wisdom and life
experience. Natalie attributes her success to her faith
and her relentlessness, and is always on the lookout for
opportunities that will both excite and challenge her.

Visit her website at www.nataliemangrum.com.

CPSIA information can be obtained
at www.ICGtesting.com
Printed in the USA
LVHW051029041119
636239LV00015B/2142/P